BUILDING WRECKING

BUILDING WRECKING

The How and Why of a Vital Industry

by JEAN POINDEXTER COLBY

Photographs by Corinthia Morss,
the author, and others

HASTINGS HOUSE PUBLISHERS

New York

Published simultaneously in Canada by
Saunders of Toronto, Ltd., Don Mills, Ontario

Library of Congress Catalogue Card Number: 72-5484
Library of Congress Cataloging in Publication Data
Colby, Jean (Poindexter) Date
    Building wrecking.

    SUMMARY: Describes the methods, machinery, workers, labor unions, and processes involved in wrecking a building.
    Bibliography: p.
    1. Wrecking—Juvenile literature. [1. Wrecking]
I. Morss, Corinthia, illus. II. Title.
TH153.C59   690'.26   72-5484
ISBN 0-8038-0746-5

Printed in the United States of America

To my friend, Kinty Morss,
for her enthusiasm and help with this project
and many others.

CONTENTS

INTRODUCTION   9

Chapter One

METHODS AND MACHINERY   11

     Hand demolition   11

     Machine demolition   16

     Demolition by blasting   34

Chapter Two

WORKERS   41

     Strippers, loaders, chauffeurs, foremen and others   41

     The crane crew: operator, oiler, tag-man   44

     Labor unions, company responsibilities   47

Chapter Three

HOW A BUILDING IS WRECKED   51

Chapter Four

    SALVAGE, VANDALISM, ECOLOGY,

    HISTORIC PRESERVATION   61

Chapter Five

    THE GROWTH OF THE

    DEMOLITION INDUSTRY   78

        Housing developments in urban and

           suburban areas   79

        Slum clearance   81

        Clearance for new freeways   83

        Buildings that have outlived their usefulness   84

    ACKNOWLEDGMENTS   89

    BIBLIOGRAPHY   91

    INDEX   92

INTRODUCTION

Across this nation and many others the big cranes of the building wrecking companies are at work. Crash! goes the huge bucket through roofs and floors. Bang! goes the big iron ball against walls. Of course, these cranes are there for the purpose of destruction, or demolition, as it is called nowadays. However, in many ways they are a sign of progress, of the world moving forward to better housing, more efficient procedures in business and manufacturing, and sometimes a return to the original beauty of the land.

A bar man at work.

CHAPTER ONE

Methods and Machinery

There are many ways to tear down a building. Sometimes several are used and sometimes only one.

Burning

The simplest way to demolish small wooden buildings such as sheds, barns and houses is to burn them. However, in most localities that is not allowed any more because the smoke pollutes the air.

Hand Demolition

Tearing apart by hand tools. Buildings have been torn down by hand ever since the first one was built. Curiously enough, the modern tool for hand demolition is very much like the tool used in colonial days for *building* houses. The old-fashioned *adze*, when expertly handled, could shape beams and boards from tree trunks. The modern *wrecking-adze* is smaller, lighter and narrower than the old one, and has a little heel on the end that serves as a hammer to knock through roofs, rotten

11

Modern tools: acetylene torch gauge, wrecking adze, wrecking bar, and hammer.

boards, or light construction of all kinds. The main blade is used to pry apart beams, planks, partitions, and so on. In some parts of the country the wrecking bar is used instead of the adze.

There are many other hand tools used in building wrecking. Some of these are common to different trades, such as the crowbar, sledge hammer, wedge and tire iron.

Also classed as demolition hand tools are the acetylene torch* and the compressed-air drill.** The torch is used to cut

---

* Acetylene is a colorless gas that burns when combined with oxygen at high temperatures. When the two gases are ignited in the torch the flame oxydizes steel into hot molten metal and blows it away.

** The compressed-air drill operates off a line that supplies hundreds of pounds of pressure. This runs a piston-operated impact mechanism of great force. Concrete can be broken up by it or dynamite loads can be planted at the bottom of the holes made by the drills. These dynamite charges are timed and often radio-controlled. This is the reason two-way radios should be turned off in their vicinity.

through metal pipes, plates and girders. It has such a hot flame that it slides through metal like a hot knife through butter, and it is a necessity in taking down large structures with steel beams like hotels, factories, high-rise apartments and bridges. Without it wreckers would take years to demolish skyscrapers.

The compressed-air drill is an essential for breaking up asphalt, concrete, brick walls, and other types of heavy masonry. It is the same drill that is often seen in the streets cutting through paving to expose sewer or utility pipes. There are many complex forms of this drill used in demolition and construction. A photograph of one type of drill, a hobknocker or jackhammer, appears on pages 14–15.

Hand demolition is always used to *start* the wrecking of large buildings. For instance, one of the first steps in taking down any substantial structure is *stripping* it. This means removing anything of value that can be reused or sold. These

A workman using an adze.

items are called *scrap* or *salvage* and will be treated in Chapter 4. They include windows, flooring, beams, bricks, pipes, plumbing fixtures, light fixtures, mantelpieces, paneling, doors, scrap metal and so on.

There is also a lot of handwork in taking down corner buildings and the walls of buildings close to the street. Windows, for instance, are either taken out or are taped, and other precautions are taken so that workmen and passers-by will not be injured. Safety codes and insurance rulings are very strict in this respect. The author and photographer often had difficulty obtaining points of vantage because of these precautions.

Machine Demolition

The biggest part of modern building wrecking today is done by machine, and the most important machine is the crane.

Cranes come in many sizes, and may be mounted on trucks, trains, tugs or ships.

The kind most commonly used in demolition moves along slowly on caterpillar treads, or is carried to the job on a long, flatbed truck. Many modern cranes have wheels and can travel under their own power.

Each crane has four parts:

1) the treads called the "cat." Like tanks in warfare, these can climb over rough land, through ditches, and down or up hills. Here is one perched on a peak in Dorchester, Massachusetts. It has only one edifice left to demolish in what was a vast industrial slum.

As mentioned, many cranes have wheels instead of treads. These are practical for city streets or flat areas near good roads.

2) the "house," which contains the motor and the cab where the operator sits behind his controls. The house is

A modern self-propelled crane with 8 wheels and 2 cabs.

mounted on a turnstyle that can swing a full circle. This enables an operator to attack his job from any angle he wishes. The modern cab is smaller than those on older cranes and is dirt and noise-proof, even heated and sometimes air-conditioned. Some of the huge modern cranes have eight or even twelve wheels and two cabs. The operator guides the crane through the streets from the one on the back. He operates the boom and the bucket or ball from the forward one.

3) the "boom" or the long neck. This varies in length from 30 to 400 feet and may be in one, two or three parts. The height and general size of the building to be razed regulate the boom used: the higher and more strongly constructed the building is, the longer the boom. A boom is usually made of

A crane with jib extended.

light, cross-hatched steel to keep its weight down but it is made to bear heavy loads. Giant cables are fed through it to:

4) the "jib." Also of cross-hatched steel, this is the small tip of the boom.

From the boom is hung the *clam shell* or *bucket*. These vary in size and shape depending on the job. They go from two tons on up in weight and are also measured by the number of cubic yards they hold.

It is interesting to note that the bucket was not used to crush buildings until the 1930's. Until then wrecking was done almost entirely by hand. Buckets were employed principally to

A clam bucket in action.

A close-up of a clam bucket.

dredge harbors and dig ditches or foundation holes. One cannot
help wonder who was the first operator to let one fall on a
house and thereby start a whole new method of building
wrecking!

Whoever did this probably thought of another use for the
bucket: biting away at a wall. Once the roof is off a house, the
bucket can swoop down, open its jaws, and bite off a huge hunk
of wood, brick, or plaster, and then turn and drop it on a pile
or in a truck, ready for removal. Or, if a building is already re-
duced to a heap of twisted wires, beams and rubble, it can pick
up a big mouthful, swing around to a truck and open wide to
disgorge it where desired. Then the truck trundles off to dump
its load in an approved place.

A pear-shaped wrecking ball being used in a search for radio-active material.

For high or very well-constructed buildings, however, a different weapon of destruction is hitched on the crane. This is called a *ball* although it actually is often pear or bottle-shaped. The ball-shaped ones go from 500 to about 5000 pounds in weight while the pear-shaped ones vary from 1500 to 12,500.

When fastened on the end of a heavy cable or chain these

A ball striking a corner post.

balls can be swung against a building with lethal effect. Most crane operators can direct them very expertly and take pride in doing so.

Here is a ball making its fourth pass at a corner post of concrete reinforced with steel rods. It took six swipes to knock it down. Note that truck tires are often suspended above the ball to absorb shock on the cables and main boom.

Almost all cranes are powered by Diesel* motors. These are slow in warming up, but they are so strong that a large Diesel-powered crane can hoist heavy machinery like front-end loaders or small, bantam cranes to the top floors of tall buildings that are being demolished. They are mostly equipped with hydraulic** controls which enable the operators to make smooth, precise swings.

Cranes, like automobiles, operate in about the same way whatever their size except for minor differences. Very modern cranes are simpler than the older models*** but by and large the inside of a cab contains four main *levers:*

1. When engaged, this controls the crawlers or treads. When disengaged, it controls the swing of the house.
2. This one controls the main *hoist*, to raise or lower the bucket or whatever is fastened to it.

* The Diesel engine was patented in 1892 by Rudolf Diesel, a German engineer. Instead of igniting fuel by a spark as in a gasoline engine, it compresses air to the igniting point. Because of the very high compression, heavy engine casings are needed but cheap fuel can be used, like crude oil. Hence the Diesel oil smell and heavy exhaust. Efforts are being made to control these.

** An hydraulic engine is one which uses the energy of water pressure to drive machinery. In this case it consists of a small piston, a large piston, and a vessel containing fluid. It operates on a principle discovered in the 1600's by the physicist, Blaise Pascal, that pressure exerted on any liquid enclosed in a vessel will create equal pressure per unit or area on everything the liquid touches. (Nowadays oil is generally used instead of water.)

*** The owner of one large wrecking company said that many modern cranes are simple and easy enough for a woman to operate. However, building wrecking is one industry women have been slow to penetrate. Freddie Loizeaux, wife of the head of Controlled Demolition, Inc. and an important executive in that company (see the next section) transports explosives frequently and hence has a blaster's license, but she is the only woman in that business so far. There are, however, other women executives in this industry.

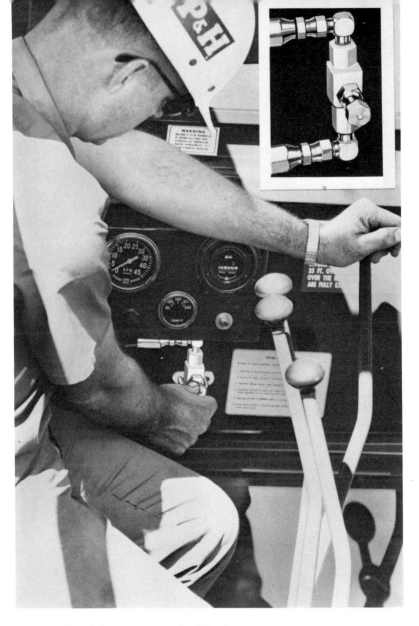

Levers and pedals in a crane cab, side view.

3. This controls the secondary hoist. It opens or closes the clam shell or bucket.
4. This controls the up and down movement of the boom.
   In front of the operator is a panel of *gauges* and *valves*.

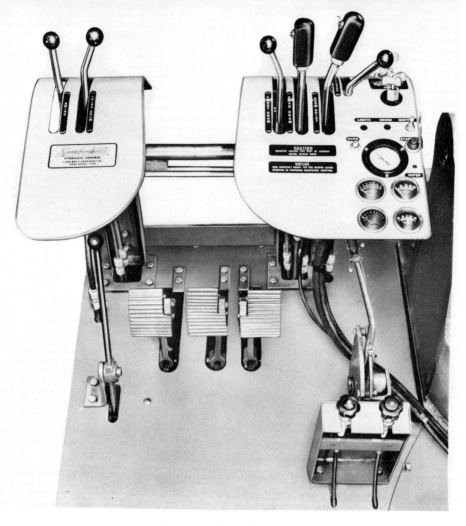

A crane operator's console in a modern cab.

To the right there sometimes is a lever controlling the swing of the ball. Actually, as in automobiles, the levers and gauges are often different depending on the make, the model and the year of manufacture of the crane.

There are always two *pedals:* a clutch and a brake, and sometimes more for other purposes.

The *cables* that travel the length of the boom are very important. They must be tested for safety and efficiency before each new job. New wire is put in frequently.

Cranes start at about 30 tons* in weight and go up to huge affairs of 300 tons that can cost $250,000 each. Being well-built, they have high resale value. For instance, a crane that cost $85,000 in 1967 was resold at $51,000 in 1972. Modern crane tires cost around $400 each and hence are protected on the work site by steel fins or outriggers that can be projected from the sides of the crane. These have short legs with round, flat steel feet which, when lowered, bear the weight of the crane body and the load it is lifting. After these feet are lowered to the ground, the wheels with their valuable tires can be raised while the work is in progress. (This move also protects the motor from the weight.) When the job is done, the wheels are lowered, the outriggers are retracted, and the crane can be moved off.

Naturally, the large cranes are a menace in traffic so they are driven to their destination at night or on weekends when

* The tonnage referred to is not the weight of the crane but what it can lift.

A crane with a retractable boom.

The first stage in demolishing a house by a dozer.

A scoop dozer holding a battering ram in its "teeth."

A front-end loader.

traffic is light. For short hauls, the booms are lowered flat; for long journeys, the front sections are taken apart and fastened on the side. Modern bantam cranes have booms made of hollow, steel sections that telescope within themselves. They can extend or retract simultaneously and are easier to move around and handle in tight places. However, the big cranes with their long booms reaching into the sky will always be the work horses of the industry.

Bulldozing. One of the new methods of wrecking small buildings makes use of the modern bulldozers and front-end loaders. Some dozers are so powerful that they can be run right through the side of a house.

Front-end loaders can smash the side of a building, scoop up the pieces with their buckets, and then lift and dump their

A scoop dozer. Note the protective helmet with visor on the operator.

loads into a waiting truck. Their long, hydraulic-powered boom arms enable them even to scoop up a pile of debris in front of them and then pass it right over the driver's head to a truck in *back* of them. A scoop dozer can also demolish and load, as the photograph on the opposite page shows.

Small pushing and scooping jobs can be done by little "bobcats" or "super-compact kittens" that are really midget dozers. Different attachments can be put on them to do different chores, like snowplowing sidewalks. Their small width (sometimes only four or five feet) enables them to go through doorways or between walls, and they are easy to maneuver.

A bobcat.

A bobcat often used to scoop off rubble on the top floors of high buildings being wrecked.

A dump trailer.

Much of the handwork of shoveling and leveling that used to consume so much time is now taken care of by these clever, versatile machines. They are very expensive but require only one operator and do the work of a dozen men at hand labor. They and other instances of mechanization and automation in the building-wrecking and construction industries certainly contribute to the rise of unemployment in the United States, but they are also one of the reasons that demolition nowadays is twice as fast as it used to be.

Last but not least in demolition equipment is the dump trailer. It is the work horse of the industry.

Before leaving the subject of wrecking machinery, it is important to note that a large and vital sub-industry has come into being—that of renting equipment. Few companies could keep a $240,000 crane busy every day. Also, ownership of all the machines used on a big job would require a lot of capital. Hence, rental companies do a rushing business leasing cranes, bulldozers, front-end loaders, back hoes (used more in construction than destruction), scaffolding and so on. For instance, a nice substantial crane and crew to go with it can be leased for about $50 to $80 an hour!

Blasting

Blasting has been a way to demolish buildings ever since dynamite was invented. Nitroglycerine, the explosive part of dynamite, was discovered in 1846. When exploded it takes up 10,000 times as much space as it does in its heavy liquid form. This is why it exerts so much force and can blow apart almost anything.

It was Alfred Nobel, a Swedish chemist and founder of the famous Nobel Peace Prize, who invented dynamite in 1867. He performed many experiments with it until he found a way to control it safely. He mixed nitroglycerine with chalky earth or other substances like wood pulp, which lowered its sensitivity to shock. He also invented the detonator cap that allowed dynamite charges to be timed and controlled.* Because of his work, dynamite was soon used extensively to open up mine shafts, expedite the digging of foundation holes, and to level old bridges and other structures.

In the last ten years the use of dynamite in demolition has increased tremendously because it is quicker and less expensive than the conventional method of ball and bucket. It is seemingly more dangerous but, according to the firms that now specialize in it, these dangers exist only in the minds of city and state safety officials who shudder at the very word *dynamite*.

According to the leading proponent of the method, John D. Loizeaux, owner of a family-run business** called Controlled Demolition, Inc. of Towson, Maryland, these fears are unfounded. He has been in business 30 years and has an impressive list of hundreds of successful demolition operations. These include hotels, warehouses, apartments, prisons, parking ga-

---

* The story goes that Nobel became so alarmed at the potential danger of his many inventions in connection with explosives, he gave the Peace Prize to compensate humanity for them.
** Freddie, John's wife, is secretary-treasurer; son Mark is vice-president; and Douglas is his father's personal assistant during his college vacations.

rages, bridges, smokestacks, transmitting towers, banks, bank vaults, grain elevators, docks, river dams, power plants . . . every kind of construction put up by man, and some that were not. (He got the idea for controlled demolition when, as a student at the University of Georgia in 1939, his forestry class helped to drill blast holes for Dupont engineers hired to reroute the Oconee River near Athens. The river's course was changed in twelve minutes and this young man awakened to the possibilities of a new business.)

Even more impressive is Loizeaux's safety record. He carries tremendously expensive insurance and he has never made a claim on it in his 30 years of business.

One reason for his success in this field is his careful preparation and planning before each operation. He works on the principle that if the props are knocked out from under a building it will fall of its own weight. The debris will not fall far or take up too much room because most structures are about 85% open space. He has proven that with enough knowledge of a building's structure and the proper placement of explosives, it can be dropped straight in on itself, or into an excavation close by. However, only tall buildings with a lot of space around them can be blasted. This open area must be roughly half the height of the building. And, if a building is less than six stories, it is cheaper to use conventional methods.

When Mr. Loizeaux is called in to demolish a building, he first asks for the blueprints so he can study the structure. If these are not available—which is usually the case with older buildings—he examines the building itself to find out where its strength lies in order to attack that area. The charges are carefully spaced there and are set off by a blasting machine.*

* The Dupont Company manufactures one called the SS-1000 Blasting Machine. The instructions are precise and give plenty of warning to the operator. Excoa (the Explosives Corporation of America) markets a Mini-Blaster, or pocket-size machine. Of course, only licensed buyers can purchase these.

Mrs. Loizeaux says, "Perhaps the real key to success in the custom dynamiting game is imagination and guts. When the charges go off they sound like a single rolling explosion to the uninitiated observer, but what really happens is that instantaneous charges go off in milli-second delays so that the noise is spread out."

Actually only a small amount of dynamite is used in order to avoid blowing the debris around and shaking surrounding buildings. Seismographs* placed on some of the largest jobs show that passing trucks often cause more vibration than the blasting.

---

* Seismometers are instruments originally invented to record tremors made by earthquakes. Seismographs trace these tremors on revolving drums and these graphs are used by companies drilling for oil as well as other industries.

The Robert E. Lee Hotel in Winston-Salem, North Carolina, before, during, and after demolition by blasting.

Two smoke stacks are blown up at the Fleischman Yeast Co. plant, Washington, D.C.

In regard to noise, Mrs. Loizeaux says, "We have not made special plans to eliminate or lessen noise because our charges make very little since most of them are below ground level. As often as feasible we use shaped charges which cause even less noise and practically no concussion as compared with old bulk charges."

As in other demolition procedures, many safety precautions are taken. As usual, all the pipes containing utilities are capped and buried under several feet of earth to absorb the shock. Doors in nearby buildings are taped to prevent dust seepage and large trailer trucks are parked in front of plate-glass windows. Of course, the company makes certain that no human beings are in or near the structure when the charges go off.

Even so, many safety and fire officials are apprehensive at the thought of explosives used in heavily populated areas. They often are reassured, though, by photographs like those preceding and by color films that are as dramatic as they are convincing. Add to all this the fact that a great deal of money and time are saved on almost any operation. For instance, a week of preparation and a few seconds of blasting demolish large buildings that would ordinarily take weeks or months to bring down. Hence, it is no wonder that Controlled Demolition, Inc. has projects lined up all over the United States. It also is no surprise that several competing companies are now in business, and more are starting.

Naturally, this form of demolition is also competition for the "bucket and ball" wrecking companies. However, some "regular" firms are subcontracting with the explosive demolition companies so they can handle more jobs. In fact, the projects of Controlled Demolition, Inc. and other similar companies are now all of the subcontract nature. The blasting experts work with a crew from the wrecking company in preparing the building, positioning the charges, and so on, and the original wrecking company clears up the site.

It does take a lot of know-how. In fact, building wrecking has become a job for trained, educated professionals who study their work and its results, take infinite pains, and do an increasingly better job. The companies using controlled explosives are very much a part of the future of the business.

CHAPTER TWO

Workers

If you watch a building being torn down in a big city, one of the first things you notice is that there are many workmen wearing different colored helmets. The colors indicate what crews the men are on and sometimes who are the bosses of those crews. The helmets themselves are for safety purposes, to protect the men from falling bricks or debris. Originally they were made of steel, but these were too hot, so now they are made of a very strong plastic. However, as one workman said, "if you're really hit, nothing will save you. That's the chance you take." (See pages 39, 44, 50, 52 for other safety measures.)

There are several kinds of crews: for instance, the *strippers or trimmers* who go in the building first and take out scrap and salvage. These men know enough about plumbing and heating to remove pipes, fixtures, radiators, furnaces, and so on with a minimum of damage. Others are adzemen or barmen who can take out floors, paneling, fireplaces, beams, and other salable objects made of wood. Not so much of this salvage work is done on big buildings now because of the empha-

Bar men at work.

sis on speed, but some material is saved (See Chapter 4). These men are paid to work fast and cannot always do careful handwork since they must prepare the building on time for the crane operators.

Other crews are *loaders* whose job it is to fill the trucks with salvage and the debris that follows the salvaged material. *Truck drivers* or *chauffeurs* are still another group. *Front-end loader* and *bulldozer operators* are still another. (There also used to be a special class called *burners*.) Then there are *compressor operators* and a foreman for each crew. In fact, there are many different kinds of workers but of them all the most highly trained and the best paid are the *crane operators*.

Workmen demolishing a large gas tank with acetylene torches. To do this, they filled the tank with water and did the work standing in rowboats. As the tank was cut down, the water was lowered.

The Crane Crew. The man who operates a crane has always had long experience. It takes years of training to run this enormous piece of machinery carefully and effectively. That ball or bucket must be operated at maximum efficiency or the wrecking company does not complete its contract on time. Also the operator must control his tremendously heavy bucket or ball with great precision for safety reasons. The lives of the other workmen, especially the loaders and crane directors, would be endangered by a green handler. It would be easy to knock a man off his perch on a wall, or to crush him with a load of bricks or rubble.

For reasons of safety and efficiency, therefore, the operator never works alone. He always has an *oiler*, a man who helps him service the machinery, who is studying to be an operator himself someday.

To give you an idea of how skilled these two men must be, they are required to take apart their crane, look over each part to be sure it is in perfect running order, service it, and reassemble it at frequent intervals. They are especially careful to test the cables before every day's work and to replace them if necessary.

On big projects the crane operator has a third man to help him: a *tag-man*. His job is to direct the work of the crane, and signal where to swing the ball or drop the bucket. He is particularly important where "end" structures are being razed. End structures are those next to buildings that are to be left standing, or close to busy sidewalks or streets.

Occasionally there are unusual incidents relating to end structures. Sometimes when a whole city block is to be taken down, a small homeowner or shopowner will hold out and will not sell to the government or the corporation acquiring the tract. It is the job of the crane operator in these cases to level

Lawrence Dewers, crane operator for the Duane Wrecking Co., Quincy, Mass.

the block of all its buildings but to leave intact, sometimes right in the middle, the small store or home that is still owned by an individual!

Some years ago one such owner was not too pleased with himself when he found that his house, the last one left in a large city block, had become a haven for all the rats whose former domiciles were no more. Two tons of vermin were killed by exterminators and then shoveled from his basement. The author, who was nearby just before the rats were gassed, will never forget the extraordinary hum of the vermin that came from the house even though all windows and doors were sealed. Nowadays there is a rule that all buildings must be "ratted" before demolition begins.

A house left alone in the middle of a demolition project.

Labor Unions, Company Responsibilities

Like most workers in the United States, demolition men belong to labor unions. The job and yard laborers, who include foremen, nail extractors, adzemen, barmen and jackhammer men, belong to the Building Wreckers Union Local, which is a division of the International Hod Carriers Building and Common Laborers Union of America. The truckdrivers belong to the A.F. of L. (American Federation of Labor) Union Local, the division of the International Brotherhood of Teamsters, Chauffeurs, or Helpers. The crane operators, oilers, front-end loader, bulldozer and compressor operators are part of the Union of Operating Engineers, the Portable and Hoisting division. All men pay dues to these unions, and to the Laborers Health and Welfare Fund of whatever state they work in. The wrecking companies also contribute to this.

If an accident occurs to a man while on the job, the insurance company pays his wages, his hospitalization and other health expenses through Workman's Compensation. In regard to pensions, the unions to which a man belongs pay toward them, and the laborer does, too. In some cases he can elect to do so or not. The retirement age is 62 and the man must have worked 25 to 30 years as a member of a union (they vary in the exact amount of time) to qualify for it.

The unions are very important in determining the wages, both regular and overtime, paid to the workers. They also lay down regulations as to hours and kind of labor. (For instance, on certain jobs a foreman can do no manual labor.)* Whenever

* Other interesting union rules are that the duties of an oiler are to grease the crane and every crane requires an oiler. This only takes a few minutes and a company cannot require anything else from this man. A compressor operator's only duties are to turn on the compressor in the morning and turn it off at night.

a contract expires—which is every three years for the engineers and the truck drivers—union officials meet with the Building Wreckers Association (the company owners) and their legal representatives to decide on the amount of the next raise. And it is almost always a raise; rarely a cut, which makes the building-wrecking business a good one to get into.

This was almost impossible to do ten or twenty years ago. There has always been a slow personnel turnover in demolition because the same men continue in the top jobs (for instance, the crane operators) for their lifetimes.

Now the possibilities of employment are a little better. Men who like outdoor work are in demand as laborers, loaders and truckdrivers, and the Portable and Hoisting Engineers Union runs apprentice schools for oilers in some cities. Also, young men with business experience can often find administrative jobs in this rapidly growing business. All new workers, however, must join the union.

Actually this tight labor situation holds true in many other fields—printing and construction, for instance. The unions control the situation except for the direct families of the owners. This is probably one of the reasons building wrecking has always been a family business. Sons or sons-in-law are apt to continue in it because it is interesting (every job is different) and profitable. They have been brought up in it and it is easier to get into than a new career. The Duane family* in Massachusetts and the Loizeaux family in Maryland are good examples.

The government is trying to break the stranglehold of the unions on building-wrecking labor by enforcing the Equal Em-

---

* The Duane Wrecking Company in Quincy, Massachusetts, started in 1919 when the grandfather of Herbert and Jack Duane decided his job on the police force was not going to support his seven children. There is a strong possibility that in a dozen or so years the fourth generation of Duanes will continue to be in the demolition business.

Two demolition contractors at the
1972 National Convention in Miami Beach.

ployment Opportunity Act. For example, this requires that a
company advertise available jobs in minority newspapers and
be impartial in interviews. Some progress has been made in
hiring blacks and there are four large wrecking companies
owned and operated by blacks. They are in Texas, Colorado,
Washington, D.C. and Detroit. There is also a wrecking company that has made a policy of hiring the handicapped since 1933.
They do piecework like cleaning off salvaged bricks and lumber.

On the whole the building-wrecking industry is trying hard to give equal opportunities to all races. Some progress has been made, and the employers are also working toward increased safety. Because the work is dangerous, the companies must carry expensive insurance on the men and try to get them to observe safety precautions. Since modern safety measures have been enforced, and machines have taken over many of the exhausting jobs, accidents and heart attacks have greatly decreased.

Partly burned buildings or "burnt jobs" are the greatest risk to wreckers. No one can tell whether floors and walls damaged by fire are safe or not. They may look all right but the supports may be seriously weakened where it does not show. The wreckers have to go in and take a chance.

So it is a risky profession, but most of the men like it. The pay is good. The work is not seasonal like other types. Right now, as one worker said, "There is no unemployment in demolition and no layoffs." Also, demolition men take pride in a good job. One crane operator said to the author, "I'm glad to have a hand in pulling down some of these old tenements. There'll be a beautiful building here by next year."

CHAPTER THREE

How a Building is Wrecked

The average building comes down fairly easily under modern building-wrecking methods, but a good deal has to go on before the first crane lumbers up to the site.

First, if it is a government project the job is advertised in the newspapers by a federal agency, or bids are requested by private concerns such as construction firms who have been hired to build on a site already occupied, or by owners of structures that have been condemned as unfit for human occupancy.

When a wrecking company's estimate has been accepted, two kinds of bonds must be posted. The first one is for performance and states that the company will do the job in such a manner to the amount of the contract. The second one is a Labor and Material Bond which guarantees that the contractor will pay for all labor and material used on the project.

Wrecking licenses are required in some states and soon will be in all. They are granted on the basis of experience and are of three kinds: 1) for wooden buildings, 2) for brick and concrete, and 3) a master's license that qualifies a company for any kind of demolition.

The tax department of the city or town has to be notified so the property to be demolished will be taken off the tax roll. The building department must be told so the building can be taken off the city or town maps.

Then in many cases, permits must be obtained from the following city departments: engineering, health, sewer, electricity, gas and fire. The first act inside the doomed building is to cap the utilities. Then the building is "ratted" by an exterminator. Often animals other than rats are discovered in it, especially if it has been vacant for a long time. A careful search is made for human boarders, too, as many a vagrant, alcoholic, or drug addict has been found in a supposedly empty building.

Safety measures required by the town or city ordinances* and the insurance company must be taken. All entrances must be blocked off, no debris left at night, and all windows taken out. Workers must wear helmets and protective shoes that nails cannot penetrate. Some cities require heavy glasses and gloves.

After a steward arrives from the union—he is the first to come and the last to go—work is begun. First, the building is "stripped" or "trimmed" for salable items, as has been explained. These include pipes, furnaces, toilet fixtures, stoves, flooring, doors, windows, and any scrap metal such as steel, iron, copper, lead and zinc. (See Salvage, Chapter 4)

Let us watch two structures being wrecked: a typical four or five-story brick building with stores on the first floor and lofts or offices on the others, and a 20-story apartment house with a stone front and concrete side walls covering half a city block.

* In Massachusetts a permit must be obtained from the Department of Labor and Industries, the Division of Industrial Safety. It is issued by an Industrial Inspector in Building Operations. He checks to see that the safety controls defined by the Occupational Safety and Health Act of 1970 have been followed.

A ball finishes off a reinforced concrete garage.

Stripping is done from the first floor *up*, but the actual building wrecking is done from the top floor *down*.

In the case of the smaller building, a medium-sized crane (say, about 35 tons) comes crawling up or is driven off a truck trailer, and the crane operator and oiler are briefed—given orders—by the foreman or boss. A two or three-ton bucket is raised on the boom of the crane and dropped through the roof. Crash! This is repeated until the roof is gone.

Then the crane takes big bites out of the walls, leveling them to the next floor. Crash! goes the bucket again through that floor and later, after the floor is gone, the bucket bites away the walls to the next floor. Interior walls are taken down at the same time.

After each bite the crane swings around and lets the contents fall into a waiting truck, one of the line of trucks that have come up while the job was progressing. As each truck is packed and filled by a loader, the chauffeur drives it off to the dump used by the wrecking company.

When the crane has picked up the big stuff, a front-end loader comes in and shovels up the rest. A bulldozer levels the ground, and after four or five hours of this crashing, crunching, biting, and loading, the building is no more.

Sometimes two buildings share a wall, and when one building goes down the inside of the next one is revealed. The sight of a slice of one of these buildings often gives the observer a strange feeling. It is like looking into a human dollhouse. Kitchen on top of kitchen on top of kitchen are open to the outdoor air with their adjoining parlors or bedrooms. Each slice has a different dirty wallpaper, different colored woodwork, perhaps ragged curtains still at the windows. How many people spent months and years in those rooms, slept, cooked, ate, argued, studied there! Now the doors flap in space, dirty bathtubs look up into the sky, and the sun enters dark corners that never saw it before. Soon that building, too, will be nothing but a memory in the minds of a few people.

Taking down the larger structure is a longer, harder job. Like the small one, it, too, is stripped, and the windows and doors taken out, but the process changes from this point on.

If it is winter, the roof is left on, the window holes are covered with sheetrock, and the walls are left standing to protect the workers from the weather. The floors are shored up, so that machinery and men will not fall through. The corners of all the retaining walls are buttressed so they won't fall in, and scaffolding is put around to secure the outside walls and provide walking space for the workers. Open elevators are put up on the outside of the building to carry up men and supplies,

An old brownstone house on Boylston Street, Boston. Each of these fireplaces was in a handsome Victorian living room.

Scaffolding on the old First National Bank Building, Boston.

The drive-in hole under a building about to be demolished.

and chutes are built in elevator shafts or outside down which brick and rubble can be thrown into the basement or into a truck to be carted away. Meanwhile all sidewalks have been covered or passers-by diverted from the scene.

At this point the first crane, probably a big tower one, say 100 tons with a 200-foot boom lying flat, enters through a hole made by hand demolition or bulldozers in a cellar or rear wall. Inside sections of flooring have been cut out to make room for the boom, often in an elevator shaft. When the crane is as-

57

The top floors of a large office building are razed. Note bobcat, lower center.

sembled, it goes to work lifting other pieces of wrecking equipment up to the floors above. These may be bantam cranes with 20 or 30 foot booms, or hobknockers for more restricted work. Dozers or bobcats are also lifted up to clear away the rubble as exterior and interior walls are demolished.

Then begins the long process of wrecking the place, floor by floor. The interior room walls come first with care taken to pull out for resale any concealed pipes, heating flues, or ducts that could not be removed by the salvage crews. After that the roof has to come off, and a crane is put to work knocking down the outside walls section by section to the next floor. Finally the floor is taken out after the machinery has gone down to the floor below. Meanwhile, in the basement or outside, trucks are busily being filled. They file loaded out of the hole in the back of the building and enter empty through another entrance in a continuous stream. Men swarm all over, apparently risking their lives every minute, but actually doing their prearranged tasks with a minimum of danger. It is a scene of order and confusion at the same time—wonderful to watch.

Eventually, nothing is left of the outside or the interior walls above the ground. The cellars and the subcellars come next, and the foundation itself. Sometimes old foundations that are in good shape are used in whole or part for the new building to be erected on the site, but mostly those, too, must be drilled apart by machine, loaded into trucks, and carried away.

One of the most difficult jobs of building wrecking beneath the ground was the case of the Hotel Marguery in New York, which was demolished to make room for the Union Carbide Building. It was discovered that this building rested on 70 reinforced concrete foundation shafts, most of them nine feet square, that went down through the tracks leading to Grand Central Station. The shafts were large to keep the structure from shaking when the trains went through, which was wise work on the part of the building contractor. But little did he realize how difficult it would be to remove those shafts! The work had to be geared to the train timetables with workmen rushing down and rushing back as commuters and other travelers shuttled in and out on the all-too-frequent trains.*

* *New York Times,* March 5, July 26, September 14, 1957

However, at long last our building is down. It took much longer, of course, than the small one—sometimes weeks or months, if done by the ball and bucket process. Nothing remains but a big hole in the ground or it may be all smoothed over. The last building-wrecking crane leaves—just as an equally big construction crane enters to change or enlarge the foundation or dig a new one. Huge trucks filled with concrete or concrete blocks and other building materials follow. The work on the new building has started. From demolition to construction in a day!

A sign in a semi-demolished building urges proprietors to lease space in the new one before the old one is down.

CHAPTER FOUR

Salvage, Vandalism, Ecology, Historic Preservation

Salvage

At first glance, it would seem that salvage, vandalism, ecology and historic preservation are four very different things. They are, but they are all tied in with demolition. Let us consider salvage first.

The original meaning of the word was the act or end results of saving a ship and its cargo from the perils of the sea. That was broadened to mean saving anything from fire, earthquakes, war or other disasters.

Nowadays salvage is a business in itself. In building wrecking, as has been explained, it consists of material that has been taken out of a building to be reused or sold. It has to be built *into* the structure—furniture, for instance, is not salvage in the building-wrecking sense.

The amount of salvage taken from a doomed building has varied with the times and the place. For instance, in the United States in the 1930's and 1940's, wrecking companies would take down structures simply for what they could get out of them in reusable or resalable material.

This situation still holds in some cases,* especially in many foreign countries, because building materials there are so scarce.

Here in the 1960's, however, there was so much government spending on demolition in urban redevelopment areas, and wages went rocketing so high that the time it took to wreck a building became more important than what was in it. Wreckers found that it was cheaper for contractors to buy new, unseasoned lumber and mix up tons of concrete than to pay men to pull the nails out of seasoned planks and boards, or clean off used bricks. Consequently, almost everything in a building to be demolished was burned or smashed and carted to the dump. Mahogany paneling, parquet flooring, marble walls, stained glass windows, ornamental iron work—who cared.

Now in the 1970's, the situation has reversed a bit although there still are companies that do not save anything. However, prices of any material that goes into a house have gone up so high that a little more attention is again given to salvage. Also, there is more interest in the past and its relics. Now, old wood, bricks, marble, ironwork and so forth are treasured.

Here are some of the items that can be bought for a fraction of their original cost at the Duane Wrecking Company storage yard in Quincy. This assortment is typical of that found at other wrecking companies over the country.**

---

* One Miami wrecker took down eight abandoned steel warehouses in 1971 on the old seaport site beside Biscayne Bay for salvage rights when the lowest demolition bid had been $77,000. He sold three of them at the halfway point but eventually lost money on the job. *Wrecking and Salvage Journal.* Jan. 1972

** On-the-spot purchases can sometimes be made before or during the wrecking process. Many valuable articles never reach the salvage lots. The unspoken rule is "finders keepers" in most instances.

Bins of nails. Some old square, hand-made ones can be found here.

Beams. Some are hand-hewn. The author is looking them over.

Left:
Stoves and hot-water heaters.

Below:
Plumbing fixtures.

The bronze tower and weathervane of the Dexter School in Brookline, Mass., is gently lowered to the ground by a crane. It will be installed elsewhere. (President Kennedy attended this school.)

A factor in the movement toward saving more material from wrecked buildings is the growing number of young married couples forced into home-ownership by high rents. A whole house can be assembled if a man has the know-how, a strong back and the time to put them all together.

Selling salvage to other industries is a bigger business than selling to individuals. Scrap metal is very much in demand. Copper, of course, sells at a premium price, as does zinc, lead and iron. The great old source for this used to be window weights. Metal prices are quoted in the *Daily Metals Report* and are fairly standard over the country. Contractors use old wooden beams for shoring up foundations or trenches, and for roof rafters. Steel beams sell quickly for many purposes. Brick is wanted for brick veneering, walls, chimneys, fireplaces and walks. It is the one salvage item that sells for more old than new because old bricks add style to any project.

Industrial companies advertise for used boilers, transformers, electric motors, pipe, structural steel, generators, conveyors—all kinds of things.

The one item, though, that was in greatest demand from building wreckers in the 1920's and even the 1930's you can't give away now: firewood.

Vandalism

Vandalism is an unfortunate part of the building-wrecking picture since many buildings have to be wrecked because they have been vandalized. Some of these were usable, occupied buildings that were so badly damaged by tenants or neighboring vandals that they were condemned by the city officials. Others were vandalized after the renters moved out, before the owners could remove the valuable or usuable fixtures from the buildings, or before new tenants could move in.

For example, a young New York architect bought a very old house built in the middle 1700's in Flushing, N.Y.. Although the house was in a run-down section, the family had taken good care of it, and it was full of handsome pine paneling, old staircases, wide floor boards and some extraordinary brass locks on many of the doors. The buyer decided, because of the poor neighborhood, to literally take the house apart and move it out further on Long Island.*

* This is called "flaking." A house is carefully cut apart, each part numbered, and put together in another spot. Many Cape Cod and other old houses have been successfully moved and reassembled in this way.

"Flaking" an old staircase. It will be lifted out whole and used in another house.

Between the time when the family moved out (noon) and the next day at 9 A.M. when the men came to flake it, everything had been taken or broken. All the lighting and plumbing fixtures were gone, the locks had been sawed off, the flooring had been torn up, even the staircases were gone and the windows had all been broken. The locks turned up in an antique store on Madison Avenue in a month or so. The owner expressed surprise when told they were stolen. She said she had bought them from a London agent who had told her they were from an English manor house. Poor old house. Poor young owner.

Below is a photograph of what is left of a Catholic school in Brookline, Massachusetts, since the school moved to another location. All windows and doors have been broken and fires started in two rooms.

Across the street the Dexter School, where President Kennedy once was a student, got the same treatment when vacated. Only the window sash remained since they were of steel. The brick buildings were so beautifully constructed that even the demolition manager said he hated to tear them down. Actually many of the window frames and the bricks were bought on the spot for very little, and the wrecker did save the beautiful oak beams in the dining room ceiling and the slate roof. The slates were carefully pried off one by one, stacked in boxes, and carried off for reuse. Slate is almost impossible to buy at any price now. So are other items in the salvage yards.

Vandalism at the St. Aidan's Parish Education Complex in Brookline, Mass.

The Dexter School, Brookline, Mass., as it looked when President Kennedy went there.

Vandalism at the Dexter School.

It is interesting to note that wreckers themselves have to guard against vandalism. Much of their machinery must be left on location and has often been ruined during the night. Now the new cranes and dozers come equipped with instrument panel covers, engine side shields and other lockup provisions.

Ecology

Twenty years ago the building-wrecking industry was one of the worst offenders in air and noise pollution. There is still room for improvement because it is hard to stifle the noise of an iron ball against a concrete foundation or eliminate the resulting dust. However, most wreckers are trying to cope with this problem. They keep a constant stream of water playing on the rubble and much of the new machinery operates at half the former noise level. Timing has been changed too so that the public will not be too much discomforted. A great deal of wrecking in dense urban areas is done on weekends even though union wages are time and a half on Saturday and double on Sunday. Of course, the noise is the same but there are not as many people to be bothered by it, and not as many to breathe the dust.

The blasting experts, as has been mentioned, contend that the noise they make is only a fraction of that from the usual wrecking methods. Certainly it does not last as long. Also they claim that, for some reason—perhaps because the buildings fall in on themselves—there is much less dust and it settles quickly.

Few industries have as great a disposal problem but progress has been made at the dumps where debris is disposed of. Incinerators with smoke-elimination devices are being installed as well as machines that compact the rubbish as much as possible.

Then, too, it is a fact that the demolition industry is probably the oldest one to recycle materials. Scrap iron, copper, lead and zinc salvaged by the demolition experts have been melted down and made into tons of usable building materials. This has always been an important part of our economy.

It is interesting to note that London is ahead of the U.S.A. in laws about polluting the air. For instance, wreckers are required to take the windows out of a building as a first step and to put up steel sheets inside each window to contain the dust within. And, in case the reader thinks Europeans never tear anything down, they do. There is a tremendous amount of demolition going on in almost all cities abroad, and they have the same problems we do: air, noise and water pollution.

Perhaps one of the best ways to meet these problems of pollution is to face them, which is what the United States building wreckers plan to do. They have a new national association* whose main purpose is to talk over matters of mutual concern. It holds yearly meetings and conferences and is thinking of convening in some European capital to swap ideas with foreign demolition experts. Something very progressive may come out of this.

On the plus side, it is important to remember that the demolition industry actually plays a necessary role in improving and beautifying our environment.

---

* The first national convention of wrecking contractors in the United States was held in January, 1972 in Miami, Florida, and was a great success. The instigator and prime mover of the event was Herbert T. Duane, Jr. He also started the only magazine in the business, the *Wrecking and Salvage Journal*, which contains news of important wrecking projects and personalities over the country. It is now in its sixth year of business and already has a nationwide circulation as well as many subscribers abroad.

Part of the Strawbery Banke Preservation Historical Project at Portsmouth, N. H., before it was cleaned up.

The Captain John Clark house at Strawbery Banke, before and after restoration. Note the new landscaping.

A row of dwellings demolished in Plymouth, Mass., to make way for new housing (opposite page).

First, you see a street of run-down tenements or multi-use houses (part house—part store, or part gas station—part tavern). The wreckers come in and tear them down, truck off the debris and level the ground. Then, according to the program agreed upon beforehand, a neat row of government housing appears. Or perhaps a park or a playground is built, or a stream previously full of weeds and beer cans is cleaned out. All this would not have been possible without demolition.

The Housing Act of 1961 provided federal assistance for the preservation of our historical heritage. Title VII of the Act included the Open Space Land Program. Its objective was to preserve open-space land for recreation, to conserve natural resources, and to improve urban appearance. In 1965 this program was expanded by the addition of an Urban Beautification Program. Part of this was to create open space for small parks on land already developed in built-up areas. It also provided funds for the removal of non-historic structures on historic sites—most of the buildings were being gradually buried in urban decay. All this called for demolition of some sort.

Historic Preservation

The building-wrecking business has gotten a bad name because many historic buildings and architectural gems have been torn down, expecially in urban development areas. This is not the fault of this particular industry. They do only what they are hired to do. For the last ten or fifteen years, however, Americans have been making a concerted effort to save buildings worth preserving. Civic organizations, historical societies, philanthropic foundations and certain generous individuals have helped tremendously, but the general public is now behind this new movement, this growing appreciation of the old. As Robert Weaver, former Secretary of HUD, said, "Never before in our history have the American people been so concerned, articulate, and moved to take action about the plight of our cities. And never before have we been so conscious of the need for discovering and preserving tangible reminders of the past.*

In 1965, in an amendment to the Housing Act of that year, federal funds were made available for the first time to save historic buildings found in HUD project areas and supply low cost loans to people to restore them. They are also available in some instances to relocate old landmarks to sites provided at cost by the government.**

* Department of Housing and Urban Development, *Preserving Historic America.* Washington, D.C., 1966.

** Not every memorable piece of architecture can be saved. Many are borderline in value. The huge old Traymore Hotel in Atlantic City, for instance, went down in spite of many efforts to save its rococo splendor. It could not be run practically any more nor could it be adapted to any other use.

The famous Bishop House, Plymouth, Mass., in transit from its original home to a new site. The public furor over the scheduled demolition of this house resulted in the Kennedy-Tower Amendment to the Housing Act of 1965. This made federal funds available for the first time to save historic landmarks found in urban redevelopment areas.

Senator and Mrs. Edward Kennedy at the Bishop House dedication.

Three colonial houses on Benefit Street in Providence, R. I., before and after restoration in the College Hill project, a demonstration study of historic area renewal.

Here are some examples of salvation and restoration on historic Benefit Street in Providence, R. I., in the College Hill Urban Renewal Project.*

In San Francisco, the Mission San Francisco de Asis in the geographic center of the city has been saved and beautified. In York, Pennsylvania, the famous Gates House and Golden Plough Tavern, two pre-Revolutionary buildings, have been restored. In Norfolk, Virginia, the old Courthouse (1850) has been returned to its pristine beauty, as have St. Mary's Catholic Church (1858) and the Moses Myer House (1792) as well as other historic structures. In Portland, Oregon, the Pittock Estate (1906) consisting of a splendid main house, caretaker's

---

* COLLEGE HILL, a demonstration study of historic area renewal, conducted by the Providence City Plan Commission in cooperation with the Providence Preservation Society and the Department of Housing and Urban Development.

lodge and 46 acres of parkland located high on Imperial Heights with a view unparalleled (they say) by any major city in the world, was acquired by money raised from public subscription, city funds, and an Open-Space Land Grant from the Urban Renewal Administration.

These are only a few of the many historic structures saved across the land. Plans to rescue hundreds more (sometimes whole areas like the Quapaw Quarter in Little Rock, Arkansas) are being formulated.*

* Another contribution by building wreckers to community life is front page news as this book goes to press. A bad fire broke out in the once fashionable Vendome Hotel in Boston on June 19, 1972 while it was being renovated into deluxe restaurants and apartments. Boston firemen, aided by men from four other communities, were fighting the blaze on the top two floors when the supports gave way, and they were catapulted into the basement and buried under tons of flaming wreckage. A call for help was sent to Herbert Duane, Jr. of the Duane Corporation, who quickly sent a large truck crane and crew to the scene, and went to superintend the operation himself. From 7 P.M. to 5 P.M. the next day the massive clam bucket lifted off burning beams and other rubble, enabling rescue operations to go on. Unfortunately nine men perished but many more would have without this masterful effort.

CHAPTER FIVE

The Growth of the Demolition Industry

Building wrecking as such has been a business for a hundred years or more. There are several companies managed now by the third generation. As mentioned, it always has been a family affair.

At first it used to be mostly a hand operation for "strong backs and weak minds," as one wrecker said, with occasional small blasts of dynamite to help things along. But buildings were built to last in the late 1800's and early 1900's, and there was no thought then that a time would come when whole city blocks would be leveled because of business expansion, high-rise apartments, or high-speed expressways.

Modern methods of building wrecking go back in some respects to England's experience in World War II.* Large parts of London and nearby Coventry were severely bombed, leaving acres of ruined or semi-ruined buildings, many more than the usual wrecking companies or wrecking methods could handle.

*Francis J. Forty, Esq., former City Engineer, Corporation of London, England.

It was a horrible situation, particularly because large numbers of people used the basements as bomb shelters. This meant that after an enemy attack the majority of dead, injured or trapped individuals were underneath the rubble, and large weights had to be moved to free them. Naturally, the emphasis was on speed to save lives rather than care to save buildings.

Britain quickly organized its home-defense forces under a Special Commissioner of Clearance. The civil authorities were also helped by the Army. Units from the Royal Engineers did a great deal of work—for instance, in the fall of 1940, 13,500 troops served for several months. They used explosives for demolition when they were sure no people were trapped inside, but most of their work consisted simply of pulling the wrecked buildings down by placing a large piece of timber inside across a window or a similar opening. A steel rope or bond was then fastened round the timber, the other end being fixed to a lorry (truck) or tank. The lorry then pulled on the rope and the weight of the timber plus the pull of the lorry collapsed the wall.*

In general, the reasons for the growth of the building-wrecking business are:

Housing Developments in Urban and Suburban Areas

World War II, as we have just seen, started the hustle that is so much a part of the business today. It showed the possibilities of mass demolition by cranes and other machinery, and even contributed a reason for the great amount of demolition that has been going on ever since. The returning troops and the

---

* During the war, the National Federation of Demolition Contractors was formed in England in 1941. They hold yearly conferences and will be joined by representatives from the American organization, the National Association of Demolition Contractors beginning with Majorca in October 1972.

79

This New England farmhouse still stands in Newton, Mass.,

tremendous number of babies born during and immediately after the war, created a serious housing shortage.

This shortage made itself felt first in the cities where suddenly there were not enough apartments or small houses to go around. Families that had been forced to live together during the war now wanted to live separately. Veterans with growing families needed more rooms. Everyone was crowded. Something had to be done.

The government started to increase its help and thus began a huge building boom here. Towns, villages and cities mushroomed. There is hardly a district near a city that does not now have its housing development—often more than one.

Before World War II a landscape might consist of a com-

but its back yard is now covered with ranch houses.

fortable farmhouse with sprawling barns, woodsheds, chicken houses and pastures.

Now, one hundred little ranch houses stand in the place of one farm, or a great estate gives way to a sea of small dwellings. Scores of families now live where one used to live. The people in the ranch houses had to have some place to go and it was better for them to move to the suburbs or into government housing than to stay in cramped living quarters where they would be uncomfortable, and unhappy.

Slum Clearance

Federal aid really started during the depression in the 1930's when the government realized that something must be done about more low-cost housing and slum clearance. The United States Housing Act of 1937 set up a U.S. Housing Authority. The Department of Housing and Urban Development was formed in 1965 and its activities really started building wrecking on the road to big business. HUD, with the assistance and approval of city and town governments, took large tracts of land by eminent domain* and had them cleared of tenements, run-down stores, warehouses, everything. Small houses or housing units were built and made available with low-cost loans. Down payments were as low as 5% of the total cost, and the monthly payments extended over a long period of time. (Previously payments had to be made quickly or the owner lost the house.)

In the 1930's some of the worst lower East Side slums in New York City were removed to make way for the clean, sunny housing of Knickerbocker Village.**

In Harlem, the black section of New York City, the housing problem has been especially acute. It is far from solved yet, but demolition and new housing projects have helped.

One huge job done by the building wreckers in New York City was the clearing of Third Avenue. The famous elevated track and stations were pulled down, and when the area was cleared, a wide boulevard was revealed. Once a dark street, bordered by saloons and secondhand stores, it is now an avenue of handsome apartment houses, office buildings, and first-class restaurants and shops.

---

* Eminent domain means the power of the state to take over private property. This has made HUD unpopular because, in spite of two supposedly fair appraisals on each piece of property, an owner always seems to feel his place is worth more than it is appraised for.
** P. 118 *Look at America*. New York City. Houghton Mifflin Co., Boston, Mass., 1948

Before we leave the changes in New York City, where buildings seem to go up and down overnight, it is interesting to note that one of the most significant and beautiful buildings in the world, the United Nations Building on First Avenue, is located on land where once droves of cattle were herded into stockyards. The whole slaughterhouse section from Forty-second Street to Forty-eighth Street was cleared by building wreckers in the late 1940's. Then the U.N. headquarters were built and a park planted with the beautiful results that so many people have seen and admired.

In the beautification process, however, many landmarks have been lost such as the Pennsylvania Station, Madison Square Garden and the Metropolitan Opera House. Many others have been threatened over the country, but as has been explained, groups of interested citizens and historical societies, helped in some instances by the Department of Housing and Urban Development, have joined together to save them.

Clearance for New Freeways

In Boston a freeway runs along the Charles River and goes around and above the North Station. On one end it connects with Storrow Drive and on the other it forks to the Mystic River Bridge and Logan International Airport. This called for a huge amount of demolition. The cranes had to raze Revolutionary brick houses and modern office buildings. Acres of slums were also cleaned up. Historic Faneuil Hall had a close shave as did Lafayette's Revolutionary offices, situated over a famous old restaurant, the Union Oyster House.

An Inner Belt has also been constructed that slices right through Boston on the old New York, New Haven and Hartford Railroad tracks. Some landmarks went down but so did some ugly factories, cheap stores, saloons and tenements. Whether the losses offset the gains in this kind of demolition must remain an unsolved question, but the facts are that traffic can get through Boston for the first time in a century. The center of the city is now open to shoppers, tourists and businessmen from other states. There is no doubt that the old town has come alive to some extent. This has happened all over America.

Buildings That Have Outlived Their Usefulness

After the static condition of business in the war years, the economy of the country began to rise in the late 1940's and early 1950's. Industries of all kinds took a new lease on life and a dramatic era of expansion and modernization resulted.

Insurance companies, banks, department and chain stores needed space for new and more efficient methods of doing business. Huge and handsome home offices for large utilities, airlines, manufacturers, and publishers were demanded and built.

An IGA store as it was in 1950 and is now (opposite page).

Even small towns were affected. The local bank on the corner with its lofty ceiling and small group of desks behind a little gate was hard to heat, had no space for computers, and the traffic pattern was wrong. The gas station at the crossroad had too few lifts for greasing and repairs, and looked old-fashioned. The grocery store had to be remodeled so the self-service shelves could be stocked from the back and more space for frozen foods provided. The churches had space, heating and acoustical problems. Why not build new ones?

Before they could do this, however, all the outmoded structures had to come down. So the building-wrecking business boomed. In the 1950's it entered a new era in which it too took advantage of government surplus, new equipment and modern revolutionary methods. The one-man companies with small crews and a few trucks gave way to big organizations owned and operated by highly trained young men who had studied the federal, state and city requirements. They talked the same language as the federal agencies, the city and town building de-

partments, and the state planning boards. They organized their work and trained their men for different jobs. They learned to live with the labor unions. Modern accounting and other business methods were introduced, and because of the enormous amount of work, the number of firms doubled and tripled. At present there are two thousand or so established demolition firms in this industry when twenty years ago there might have been three hundred. The industry is now recognized for the important role it plays in the nation's economy and its sociological future.

Examples of the wide range of work in this building-wrecking future may be glimpsed by the following headlines in recent issues of the *Wrecking and Salvage Journal.*

STUDY GROUP PROPOSES MASSIVE REBUILD FOR
HARTFORD; INITIAL COST: $780 MILLION

RAZE OR REHABILITATE 40,000 BUILDINGS IN
L.A. AREA BY 1980

150 DERELICT BUILDINGS MARKED FOR DEMO
IN DULUTH

NORFOLK, VA. KNOCKS OFF 101 BUILDINGS
IN MONTH

ST. LOUIS LAUNCHES DEMOLITION BLITZ—
4,000 DERELICT BUILDINGS TARGET

LARGE SCALE DEMOLITION IN $11 MILLION
BUFFALO PROJECT

And so it goes.

New York and other big cities in the United States have changed tremendously in the last 40 years. It is obvious that

A church being demolished in the Boston area to make room for an
expressway.

they will change more very soon. Small ones will, too. "You'd never know it," is a common remark to anyone who has been away from his home town for ten years or more. You can hardly walk a mile on city streets without seeing half-wrecked buildings with cranes working away behind the scenes, or long stretches of temporary walls studded with little window openings through which the curious can watch the fascinating process. This is a good public relations effort on the part of the demolition experts. Some companies even add a touch of humor to the rather depressing business. One wrecker, T. M. Burgin, who was razing a local movie theatre put up on the marquee:

```
*****************************************
*                                       *
*  NEXT ATTRACTION: T. M. BURGIN—       *
*          DOING HIS THING              *
*                                       *
*****************************************
```

Another has as his company's motto:

MAKING WAY FOR TOMORROW.

Perhaps that is a good way to end this book because that is just what the building wrecking companies are doing—making way for tomorrow—all over the country.

ACKNOWLEDGMENTS

I am grateful to Mr. and Mrs. Herbert T. Duane, Jr., publishers of the *Wrecking and Salvage Journal,* and to Mr. Alden S. Wood, editor, for their interest and assistance in supplying information and back copies of their journal for my use. They also were kind enough to read this book in manuscript form. Mr. Duane is president of the Duane Corporation in Dorchester, Massachusetts.

I also am indebted to Mr. Herbert T. Duane, Sr., and his staff at the John J. Duane Wrecking Co. in Quincy, Massachusetts, for allowing me on location at many of his wrecking projects and supplying me with information on the many facets of building wrecking.

Many thanks to Mr. and Mrs. John Loizeaux of the Controlled Demolition Co., Inc. of Towson, Maryland, who were most generous with information on the blasting method of demolition and their many fascinating projects.

89

I appreciate the interest and assistance of Mr. and Mrs. Warren Milliken of Plymouth, Massachusetts, in supplying information and photographs of the demolition in the HUD project area, and the moving of the historic Bishop House to its new site.

The following companies have been generous with material on and photographs of their different kinds of building-wrecking equipment: the Allis Chalmers Co., Link Belt Co., Witt-Armstrong Equipment Co., Wabco Construction Equipment Co., International Harvester, Hendrikson Manufacturing Co., CMI/Champion Manufacturing Inc., and the Vulcan Iron Works.

The Plymouth, Massachusetts, Redevelopment Authority kindly allowed me to use photographs from my book, *The Death and Rebirth of an Ancient Area,* and Strawbery Banke, Inc. in Portsmouth, New Hampshire, supplied some excellent photographs of the restoration of this beautiful old section.

BIBLIOGRAPHY

Calkins, Carroll C. "In Providence: Benefit Street Still True to Its Name." *House Beautiful* (August 1965).

Colby, Jean Poindexter. *The Rebirth of an Ancient Area.* Washington, D. C.: Department of Housing and Urban Development, 1971.

————. *Tear Down to Build Up.* New York: Hastings House, 1960.

Engineering Record. New York: McGraw Hill (1957–1972).

Hilton, Suzanne. *How Do They Get Rid Of It?* Philadelphia: Westminster, 1970.

Irvin, Hilary Somerville. "Benefit Street, Providence." *National Antiques Review* (May 1970).

Look Magazine, Editors of, in collaboration with Frederick Lewis Allen. *Look at America: New York City.* Boston: Houghton Mifflin, 1948.

May, Roger B. "Blast It Away, Boys!" *The Wall Street Journal* (March 6, 1972).

The New York Times. March 4, 1957; July 26, 1957; September 15, 1957; March 20, 1972; April 1, 1972.

Wrecking and Salvage Journal. Hingham, Massachusetts (January 1970–June 1972).

INDEX

Acetylene torch, 12, 43
Adzemen, 41, 47
American Federation of Labor, Union Local, 47
Allis Chalmers. Co., 90
Athens, Ga., 35
Atlantic City, N. J., Traymore Hotel, 74 fn

Backhoes, 33
Ball, 22, 23, 26, 34, 39, 53, 60
Barmen, 10, 41, 42, 47
Battering ram, 28
Benefit St., Providence, R. I., 76, 77
Biscayne Bay, Florida, 62 fn
Bishop House, Plymouth, Mass., 75, 89
Black-owned companies, 49
Blasting, 34, 35, 37, 39
Bobcat (dozer), 31, 32, 58
Bonds, posted, 51
Boom (a crane part), 18, 20, 23, 25–27, 29, 31
Boston, Mass., 55, 56, 77 fn, 82 fn, 83, 84, 87

Brookline, Mass., Dexter School, 64, 67, 68; St. Aidan's, 67
Bucket, 20, 21, 24, 25, 29, 34, 39, 53, 60, 77
Buffalo, N. Y., 86
Building occupants, 52
Building Wreckers Association, 48
Building Wreckers Union Local, 47
Bulldozing, 29, 54
Burgin, T. M., 88
Burners, 42
Burning, 11

Cables, 26, 27, 44
Cape Cod, Mass., 65 fn
Capt. John Clark House, Portsmouth, N. H., 71
Cat (a crane part), 16
Chauffeurs, 42, 54
Clam bucket (or clam shell), 20, 21, 25, 29, 34, 39, 53, 60, 77
CMI/Champion Manufacturing, Inc., 90
College Hill Urban Renewal, Providence, R. I., 76 fn, 77

Compressed air drill, 12, 13
Compressor operators, 42, 47
Controlled Demolition, Inc., 24 fn, 34, 39, 89
Coventry, England, 78
Cranes, 16, 18, 19, 22–27, 29, 54, 57, 58, 60, 69, 77, 88
Crane operators, 42, 44, 47, 48, 50, 53
Crawlers, 24

Daily Metals Report, 64
Department of Housing and Urban Development, 74, 76, 82, 83
Department of Labor and Industries, Division of Industrial Safety, 52 fn
Dewers, Lawrence, 45
Dexter School, Brookline, Mass., 64, 67, 68
Diesel motors, 24
Diesel, Rudolf, 24 fn
Disposal problems, 69
Dorchester, Mass., 16, 89
Dozer, 28, 31, 33; operators, 42, 47, 69
Drive-in hole, 57, 59
Duane Corporation, 77 fn, 89
Duane, Herbert T., Jr., 48 fn, 70 fn, 77 fn, 89
Duane, Herbert T., Sr., 89
Duane, Mrs. Herbert T., Jr., 89
Duane, Jack, 48 fn
Duane Wrecking Company, 45, 48 fn, 62, 89
Duluth, Minn., 86
Dump trailer, 32, 33
Dupont Company, 35
Dynamite, 34–36

Ecology, 61, 69
Elevators, 54
Eminent domain, 82
England, 78, 79 fn
English Manor House, 66
Equal Employment Opportunity Act, 49
Equipment rental, 33
Explosives Corporation of America (Excoa), 35 fn

Faneuil Hall, Boston, Mass., 83
Flaking, 65 fn, 66
Fleischman Yeast Co., 38
Flushing, N. Y., 65
Forty, Francis J., Esq., 78 fn
Front-end loader, 29, 33; operators, 42, 47

Gates House, York, Pa., 76
Golden Plough Tavern, York, Pa., 76
Grand Central Station, 59

Hand demolition, 11, 13, 16, 18
Handicapped workers, 49
Harlem, N. Y. C., 82
Hartford, Conn., 86
Helmets, 30, 41, 52
Hendrikson Manufacturing Co., 90
Historic Preservation, 61, 72, 74
Hobknocker, 15, 58
Hoist, 24, 25
Hotel Marguery, N. Y. C., 59
Houghton Mifflin Co., Boston, Mass. 82 fn
House (a crane part), 16
Housing Act of 1961, 72
Housing developments, 79

Hydraulic engine, 24

Imperial Heights, Portland, Oreg., 77
Industrial Inspector, 52 fn
Inner Belt, Boston, Mass., 83
International Brotherhood of Teamsters, Chauffeurs, and Helpers, 47
International Harvester, 90
International Hod Carriers Building and Common Laborers Union of America, 47

Jackhammer, 16; men, 47
Jib (a crane part), 19, 20

Kennedy, Mrs. Edward
Kennedy, President, 64, 67, 68
Kennedy, Sen. Edward, 75
Kennedy-Tower Amendment
Knickerbocker Village, N. Y. C., 82

Laborers Health and Welfare Fund, 47
Labor Unions, 47
Lafayette's Revolutionary Offices, Boston, Mass., 83
Licenses granted, 51
Link Belt Co., 90
Little Rock, Ark., Quapaw Quarter, 77
Loaders, 54
Logan International Airport, Boston, Mass., 83
Loiseaux, Douglas, 34 fn
Loiseaux family, 48
Loiseaux, Freddie (Mrs. John) 24 fn, 34 fn, 36, 39, 89
Loiseaux, John D., 34, 35, 89

Loiseaux, Mark, 34 fn
London, Eng., 66, 70, 78 fn
Long Island, N. Y., 65
Look at America. New York City 82 fn
Los Angeles, Cal., 86

Machine demolition, 16
Madison Ave., N. Y. C., 66
Madison Square Garden, N. Y. C., 83
Metropolitan Opera House, N.Y.C., 83
Miami, Florida, 62 fn, 70 fn
Miami Beach, Florida, 49
Milliken, Mr. and Mrs. Warren, 89
Mini-blaster, 35 fn
Mission San Francisco de Asis, San Francisco, Cal., 76
Moses Myer House, Norfolk, Va., 76
Mystic River Bridge, Boston, Mass., 83

Nail extractors, 47
National Association of Demolition Contractors, 79 fn
National Convention of Demolition Contractors, 49, 70 fn
National Federation of Demolition Contractors, 79 fn
Newton, Mass., 80
New York City, 59, 82, 83
New York Times, 59 fn.
Nitroglycerine, 34
Nobel, Alfred, 34; Peace Prize, 34
Norfolk, Va., 86; Courthouse, 76; Moses Myer House, 76; St. Mary's, 76

Occupational Safety and Health Act of 1970, 52 fn
Oconee River, Georgia, 35
Oilers, 44, 47 fn, 53
Open Space Land Program, 73, 77

Pascal, Blaise, 24 fn
Pedals, 26
Pennsylvania Station, N. Y. C., 83
Pensions, 47
Permits required, 51
Pittock Estate, Portland, Oreg., 76
Plymouth, Mass., 72, 75, 89; Redevelopment Authority, 90
Pollution, 69, 70
Portland, Oreg., Pittock Estate, 76
Portsmouth, N. H., Strawbery Banke, 71, 90
Preserving Historic America, 74 fn
Providence, R. I., Benefit St., College Hill, 76, 77; City Plan Commission, 76; Preservation Society, 76

Quincy, Mass., 45, 48, 62

Ratting, 46, 52
Recycling, 70
Retirement, 47
Risks involved, 50
Robert E. Lee Hotel, Winston-Salem, N. C., 37
Royal Engineers, 79

Safety measures, 50, 52
St. Aidan's Parish Educational Complex, Brookline, Mass., 67
St. Louis, Mo., 86

St. Mary's Catholic Church, Norfolk, Va., 76
Salvage, 59, 61–63, 65, 67
San Francisco, Cal., Mission San Francisco de Asis, 76
Scaffolding, 35, 54, 56
Scrap, 16
Seismographs, 36
Seismometers, 36
Slum clearance, 81
SS-1000 Blasting Machine, 35
Storrow Drive, Boston, Mass., 83
Strawbery Banke Preservation Historical Project, Portsmouth, N. H., 71, 90
Stripping, 13, 41, 52, 53, 54

Tag-men, 44
Third Avenue, N. Y. C., 82
Towson, Md., 34, 89
Traymore Hotel, Atlantic City, N. J., 74 fn
Trimmers, 41

Union Carbide Building, N. Y. C., 59
Union of Operating Engineers, Portable and Hoisting Division, 47, 48
Union Oyster House, Boston, Mass., 83
Union rules, 47
United Nations Building, N. Y. C., 83
United States Housing Act, 82
United States Housing Authority, 82
University of Georgia, 35
Urban Beautification Program, 73
Urban Renewal Administration, 77

Vandalism, 61, 65–69
Vendome Hotel, Boston, Mass., 77 fn
Vulcan Iron Works, 90

Wabco Construction Equipment Co., 90
Washington, D. C., Fleishman Yeast Co., 38
Weaver, Robert, 74
Winston-Salem, N. C., Robert E. Lee Hotel, 37

Witt-Armstrong Equipment Co., 90
Wood, Alden S., 89
Workman's Compensation, 47
World War II, 78–80
Wrecking adze, 11, 12, 13
Wrecking and Salvage Journal, 62 fn 70 fn, 86
Wrecking bar, 12

York, Pa., Gates House, 76; Golden Plough Tavern, 76